FRESH OUT OF THE BOX

Volume 3

Digital Worship Experiences for
Advent and Christmas

D1715928

FRESH OUT OF THE BOX
VOLUME 3

Digital Worship Experiences
for Advent and Christmas

This book is printed on acid-free, recycled paper.

Cataloging-in-publication information applied for with the
Library of Congress

ISBN 0-687-036720

Contents

Introduction

How to Use This Book and DVD

In the dark of night, Nicodemus came to Jesus seeking spiritual counsel. He sensed in Jesus the possibility of new life. Jesus' surprising answer was that Nicodemus needed to be "born anew." He invited Nicodemus to explore the possibility of living his life "fresh out of the box." This invitation required Nicodemus to re-examine his traditional assumptions and ways of doing things.

When we as the church re-examine our ways of worship, our tendency is to find something that works, box it up and label it "contemporary." Eventually, as the culture around the church changes, contemporary becomes tradition and tradition becomes stale. Worship traditions and forms need continual refreshing. The purpose of this book is to create worship that is fresh out of the box for the people of your community.

Just as Jesus invited Nicodemus to discover a fresh spirit in continuity with the tradition of Israel, so these youth worship experiences explore new ways that the Holy Spirit may be present today. They recast traditional worship in forms that grow out of digital culture. Our hope is that through these suggestions God may restore dimensions of worship that need to be born anew.

These "fresh out of the box" worship experiences grow out of specific biblical stories. Each of the ten experiences in this volume contains a series of elements that may be formed together to create an effective worship experience for our digital culture. The experiences do not exhaust creative potential. Some lack various elements such as movie suggestions, drama suggestions, and LumiClips. Others have two, three, or up to ten of each. The components depend on the creative needs of each story.

We recommend that you share the experience you intend to implement with your worship team(s) prior to planning your worship experiences together. The synergy that results from brainstorming as a group will generate more ideas, and more indigenous ideas, than can be listed here. Each *Fresh Out of the Box* experience should become a product of your own creativity and communicate to your particular culture.

The task of creating authentic, meaningful worship experiences for digital culture is more difficult than simply imitating what you see in an outline of worship. Although the individual elements help to create a powerful sense of God's presence, smooth transitions are essential for keeping people engaged in the worship experience. In public speaking, studies have shown that when the people are "lost" to the message, it takes twenty minutes or more to bring them back. Further, we live in a non-linear world. Thus we are used to "multi-tasking," engaging in multiple stimuli at once.

Because of this, we encourage you to fill the gaps between the listed elements. For example, playing the call to worship video and then closely following with the spoken word, overlapping elements in the process, is one way to remove a gap. Other ways include drawing music out under a speaker and projecting the primary worship image or a series of images between song and speaker. Be creative and see everything through the eyes of a searching but skeptical seeker who doesn't understand mediocrity or unexplained ritual.

We intentionally did not include an order to the elements. Their structuring is up to you and is dependent on the nature of your church community and any additional elements related to the theme that you might include. As a helpful aid, we have provided a sample liturgy to assist you in creating worship order. This order is based on "Eye on the Sky."

Sample Order

Opening Music—"Tower" by Cary Peirce, performed by the band with the primary graphic on the screen.

Call to Worship—As the song ends, lights down. Play the LumiClip video of the stargazers. At the end of clip, project the graphic on the screen and lights up on worship leader, who gives the call to worship.

Songs—With words on screen, the minister of music leads the congregation in two songs: "Come, Now Is the Time to Worship" and "Hail to the Lord's Anointed."

Interlude—As the second song ends, lights down and dissolve to black on the screen. Up on one of the clips from the film, *Contact.* The clip is fifty-two seconds long and illustrates how some of us spend our whole lives keeping our eyes on the sky.

Scripture/Drama/Prayer—As the clip ends, lights up on the storyteller (who is positioned stage left or right, away from the drama team). The storyteller dramatically reads the story from Matthew 24:36-44. At the end of storytelling, lights down and up on the drama team, center stage. The suggested drama summarizes the passage and invites members of the congregation to discover their own feelings relating to waiting and readiness. After the drama, the worship leader leads the prayer.

Feature Music/Offering—As the prayer ends, the music leader conducts the offering accompanied by the song, "Waiting for a Star," by Boy Meets Girl. The main graphic continues on the screen.

Sermon—The worship leader talks about the need for followers of Jesus to remain alert for signs of the coming of the kingdom of God. Use the other *Contact* clip during the message.

Closing Words—The worship leader reminds individuals that

Jesus tells us to keep our "eye on the sky," and encourages them to stay alert for the movement of God's spirit. Give the benediction while the band plays "Lift Up Your Heads."

These are only one of many options for how to develop structure for digital age worship. Avoid creating patterns that only require inserting the different songs and media into the same format each week; use the story to generate creative elements that keep the digital liturgy fresh.

For more on creating worship for our digital era, including a basis for a narrative approach to worship, read *Digital Storytellers: The Art of Communicating the Gospel in Worship* (Abingdon Press, 2002).

For assistance with configuring technology for your sanctuary and other issues related to creating media ministry, read *The Wired Church: Making Media Ministry* (Abingdon Press, 1999).

Overview

We have included a set of suggestions related to each worship experience as starting points for your own service. Though not intended to be a complete or all-inclusive preparation guide, these notes provide potential avenues as you develop your own indigenous experience.

Graphics

Each experience comes with three primary graphic images. Together they will provide the basic needs for an integrated worship experience. They are:

Main Image

This image is intended to be the primary graphic image displayed throughout your worship experience. Think of it as a default title image that can fill the visual "holes" in worship. By this we mean that there is no need for your screen to be blank at any time. The "default image" can provide smooth transitions between elements in worship. For example, when the call to worship has finished and the musicians are on their way to their instruments, you could put the graphic up to divert your congregation's attention away from the setup and keep it focused on the worship experience as this transition takes place.

Song Background

This second image is a blurred, low-contrast version of the main image. It will separate well from text that is placed on top of it. Lightly colored fonts will also help legibility in most cases, but if the image is light, use dark fonts. It is intended that this graphic be used with large bodies of text. We suggest that you use it for song lyrics, scriptures, responsive prayers, and anything else with more than two lines.

Main Image with No Words

This image has been included so that you can add your own custom sermon points, as well as add any additional illustrations that you may have. If you have lots of text to lay over the image (like a scripture) it would be best to use the song background.

All graphics are downloadable from the DVD in .bmp format. BMP, or bitmap, is a high-quality screen resolution cross-platform format. Images are approximately one megabyte each. BMP images may be inserted into any number of presentation software applications, including PowerPoint, Prologue, and Song Show Plus.

Fonts

When you start to customize your screen graphic files you'll need to pick a secondary font for the larger bodies of text. If you are an experienced graphic designer, you're probably aware of the difference between display and body fonts, but here is a quick explanation.

Display fonts (sometimes called headline fonts) are designed to draw attention to your headline (thus the name headline font) or other important copy lines and are usually more artistically complex. The font used to communicate the theme on each graphic is typically a display font. Display fonts are used for small areas of copy, such as sermon points and sub-points. They are not easily read in large blocks of text.

Body fonts (sometimes called copy font) are designed to be easy to read in larger blocks. Body fonts are also easier to read when smaller (like the font that you're reading now). A good rule of thumb for point size is to not go below 28-30pt on screen. Any font starts to look like hieroglyphics when reduced below 28pt. (There are always exceptions to the rule.) You will probably want to use your body font for your scriptures, song lyrics, and any additional information that you want to include on the screen.

Laying out song lyrics and scriptures can be trickier than you may think. You will find that there is a "happy medium" for font creativity and font size that you must determine. Picking a font that is too artistically creative will leave your congregation frustrated as they try to read song lyrics. Picking a font that is too simple, like Helvetica, can make your screen text less effective. A "dull" font will stand out from the graphics that you've acquired. By that we mean that your text may not look as integrated into the artwork we've provided. Size also can make screen text baffling, as we've stated above. One last note: Be consistent with font size. Choose one point size that will accommodate all of your graphic text screens.

Overall, seek an artistic plateau with your text layout, but don't lose sight of what you are trying to do through these graphics. It is best to make your design clear and easy to read.

Movie Suggestions

The included movie suggestions primarily feature major release (secular) motion pictures, such as those at your local theater. These movies both address and respond to the basic felt needs of our culture and are a primary way to understand and speak the gospel today. Any potentially controversial elements in the clip are noted. Since different standards of acceptability apply to different worship styles, we include a broad range of possibilities, including "R"-rated movies. Although we don't include clips with obvious violence, sexuality, or language, we recommend you review each clip prior to its use in worship. Edited versions may be available (see below).

Use of movie clips in worship requires copyright release. For more information about the legality of playing movie clips in worship and to obtain release, see the copyright section later in this introduction.

Each suggestion in the movie section of an experience lists the name of the movie, its DVD chapter and time, its VHS counter time in minutes and seconds, a description of the clip, and its length. DVD numbers work automatically; for VHS videocassettes, reset your minutes and seconds counter following the previews and warning slates and before the studio logo that starts the film.

We recommend DVDs if possible for playback. With random access, clip cueing is much more exact, thereby decreasing the probability of accidentally playing the wrong portion of the movie (which, depending on the film, could lead to very bad results). DVD players are now about the same price as VHS players. Many have "A-B" functions that allow the user to isolate the intended portion of the film, which is a great safety measure against inappropriate imagery or dialogue in worship.

If time permits, pre-cue the clip. Memorize or write down incue and outcue points, either by referencing dialogue or visuals. These clues will assist in making more effective transitions.

Lower the lights as much as possible during the playing of the clip, then raise them afterward. It is as important to create a theatrical atmosphere for viewing the clip as it is to keep your sanctuary well lit during worship.

Play both movie clips and LumiClips from their best possible source. This is both the most legal and the highest fidelity option for playback. Avoid using remotes to play the clip, which can fail at the critical moment.

As with other elements, be intentional about integrating movie clips into the broader experience. For example, create tag lines that lead into the clip. A tag line is not "let's watch the screen," but rather something that contextualizes what the congregation is about to see and provides a cue to the media crew to play the clip. In addition, adjusting the lighting lower during the clip removes distractions and broadens its impact.

Music Suggestions

As with film clips, we try to provide a broad range of music suggestions, including contemporary praise songs, hymns, youth songs, and secular hits. Each suggestion includes the name of the song, its artist(s), and notes about its use.

All songs may be performed in worship without violation of copyright so long as the song is not reproduced in written form in any way, including screen projection of lyrics, bulletin printing, etc. See the copyright section below for more details.

Many of these suggestions have sheet music available through your local music retailer. Another common method of learning the songs is by ear from their original recordings, if your band is sufficiently talented!

Integration Suggestions

The integration suggestions include a series of scripts and ideas for weaving the theme and metaphor of the experience together. These ideas include interpretive notes, call to worship scripts, prayer ideas and scripts, drama ideas, closing word/benediction scripts, and display suggestions.

Each experience contains a developed set of interpretive notes, or "sermon starters." These notes identify clues in the text about the dynamics of the original telling and hearing of the story itself. They will provide direction for experiencing the scripture first hand, rather than through a detached analysis of its theological, doctrinal meaning. You can develop these ideas in whatever way will be most helpful to your congregation. Our focus is on giving a base, formed out of the narrative experience, while staying true to the character of the Gospel.

Calls to worship may include either sample scripts or suggestions for writing your own scripts. They usually include reference to specific media—either movie clips, LumiClips, or graphics—for the call to worship is one of the best times to incorporate the use of media. In any event, use words that are authentic to you and your community. Make it real in order to communicate effectively, but keep the focus integrated through the basic metaphor for the theme.

As with all elements, seamless transitions are important. We encourage you to fill the gaps between the listed elements. A fast pace is not mandatory, but gaps between elements tend to make worshippers stop and wonder who isn't doing his or her job. One way to remove a gap is through overlapping elements, such as with the call to worship video and spoken text. For example, begin speaking while the video and/or audio is still playing, and then fade out the clip to the primary worship image under the spoken call to worship. Other ways include drawing music out under a speaker and projecting the primary worship image or a series of images between song and speaker. Be creative.

In the drama portion we have provided you with ideas for developing your own drama script. In our experience, we have learned that dramas are effective when they are indigenous, using language and references specific to your church and community. We hope our seeds will give you the base to build your own sketch.

Integration also extends to your environment. A well-developed setting for worship includes such things as color, lighting (often the two are combined), and the display of artifacts. We have included suggestions for these.

Bulletin Images

To more fully integrate the theme, you may choose to use the primary graphic as a bulletin cover image. This should be positioned prominently on the front page of your service bulletin. Font size and selection should closely match the theme's style. Any standard desktop program should be sufficient for integrating the bulletin image.

Using the Screen

The screen components provide a variety of elements for forming your own media matrix for worship. The possibilities are countless, but a few principles are important:

• In mixing your worship components together, use the screen elements as a means to transition between components in the experience. For example, run a few graphics or a small animation, if included, after the "feature music" and before the sermon.

• Overlap the call to worship video and live script with music that trails off while the worship leader begins speaking.

• If nothing else, keep the primary image up all the time. Avoid going to black. The image, like stained glass and many other art forms before it, serves a meditative function in worship.

• When customizing the image for song lyrics and other text functions, stay with similar colors and font selection. Be detailed in your approach.

• Use the enclosed media and suggestions to create references to the theme throughout the worship experience. Avoid making the first half of the service integrated and the sermon something completely different. To assist with this, use terminology related to the metaphor throughout the experience. Also refer to the interpretive notes included in the package.

Ownership

Each worship experience in this volume is an original creation of Lumicon Digital Productions. They are designed from scratch to meet your needs in today's digital culture. Purchase of this book grants you permission to use all copyrighted materials in your worship.

Each of the enclosed worship experiences was originally part of an online worship subscription created by Lumicon. These materials are designed to create an integrated experience of God in worship by using a variety of media including videos, graphics, animations, feature film clips, contemporary Christian and secular music, and creative scripts for calls to worship, prayer, and much more. Each experience is developed around a specific Scripture and tied to both theological themes and relevant topics. They are also developed in conjunction with the Revised Common Lectionary.

The authors may be contacted at Lumicon.org.

Copyright

(Excerpted from *The Wired Church: Making Media Ministry*, by Len Wilson. Nashville: Abingdon Press, 1999, pp. 158-160.)

Probably the most confusing and rumor-laden aspect of media in church life surrounds the issue of copyright. Truly, the issues are straightforward as they apply to worship and educational settings within the context of the church and community.

The basic applicable legal code is buried under Section 110 of the 1976 Copyright Act (17 U.S.C. §110[3]). Section 110 states that, without fear of breaking the law, churches may.

• Perform non-dramatic literary or musical works and religious dramatic and musical works.

• Display individual works of a non-sequential nature (17 U.S.C. §101) during services at a house of worship or other religious assembly.

"Display," as defined in legalese, means to "show a copy of [a work] either directly or by means of a film, slide, television image, or any other device or process or, in the case of a motion picture or other audiovisual work, to show individual images non-sequentially."

Translated into common English, this means churches may:

• Perform contemporary songs, regardless of the owner/copyright holder.

• Show any still image, regardless of its source, and even show frames of a film, if they are not in sequence, during worship. This includes scanned images of any sort, including newspaper headlines, periodicals, pictorial books, or whatever you dream up.

What churches may NOT do during worship, according to Section 110(3):

• Show any (pre-copywritten) motion picture, video, or audio-visual work in its entirety or by segment, as this is neither a non-dramatic nor musical work, nor is it "displayed" (according to the non-sequential definition above).

• Record programs from broadcast television, then show them in worship, as this involves both the illegal duplication of a copywritten work, and the display of sequential images.

• Synchronize any non-live or live performed recording of a musical work, for example from CD or cassette tape.

• Reproduce lyrics in any fashion from a copyright-protected musical work, including display of lyrics within projected graphic images and printing of lyrics in bulletins or other forms, including screens.

Further, Section 110(1) makes the same applications for media use in non-profit educational environments.

Outside of worship and the classroom, things get much grayer. This includes posting of works on the Internet, and sale of works to other churches or individuals. Much is made of the exemption in the copyright law for fair use. When contemplating if something may be qualified as fair use, keep the following guidelines in mind:

• The more creative a work, the less likely it is to be covered by the fair use clause.

• Although no specific percentages apply, the more of a work that is used, the less chance it is covered by fair use.

• The impact of usage on a work's market value; the more it decreases its value, the less likely it is to be fair use.

As a rule, never use fair use in a blanket way.

The only activities covered in a blanket way by fair use, according to standard interpretations of the First Amendment, are news reporting, research, and criticism. Anything else should be determined on a work-by-work basis.

This applies even to parody, one aspect of the fair use clause. Instances in which parody may suffice as a defense of potential audio-visual copyright violation might include the use of pre-recorded music with original dramatists, as in a skit or video version of a skit or TV show. However, be sure to check with a copyright lawyer on a case-by-case basis.

Fortunately, licenses exist for churches to circumvent the inability to show motion pictures and display song lyrics, two staples of a church that uses digital media. These include:

1. CCLI, or Christian Copyright Licensing International, 17201 N.E. Sacramento, Portland, OR 97230. (800)-234-2446. For permission to display song lyrics.

2. CVLI, or Christian Video Licensing International, a division of Motion Picture Licensing Corporation, P.O. Box 66970, Los Angeles, CA 90066. (800) 462-8855. The CVLI license offers umbrella permission for a number of studios available for a small yearly fee (not more than $200) to cover films already available for rental.

3. Criterion Pictures, (800)-890-9494.

4. Swank Motion Pictures, 201 S. Jefferson Avenue, St. Louis, MO 63103-2579. (800) 876-5577.
   Hyperlink http://www.swank.com/comprevid.html
   www.swank.com/comprevid.html. In addition to covering studios not covered elsewhere, Swank offers copies with license

for public exhibitions of films not yet available for rental. They also offer edited (airline) versions of films which have such versions.

For further information, consult *A Copyright Primer for Educational and Industrial Media Producers*, 2nd Edition, by Esther S. Sinofsky, and a local copyright lawyer.

Eye on the Sky

Overview

Stay awake and keep alert, for God is coming.

Theme

Eye on the Sky

Metaphor/Image

Shooting star

Treatment

Like waiting for a shooting star, we are called to watch for the sudden, joyous occasion of God's coming kingdom.

Human Need

Everyone has a need for security because of trepidation about the future's uncertainties.

Experience

That people will adopt a spiritual attitude of attentiveness.

Word

Primary Scripture: Matthew 24:36-44

Lectionary Week

First Week of Advent, Year A; Isaiah 2:1-5, Psalm 122, Romans 13:11-14

Related Scripture

Matthew 26:36-45, Genesis 6:5-9:17

Topics

Primary Topics

Advent, life of Jesus, indifference, alertness, perseverance

Related Topics

security, salvation, attentiveness, end times

Movies

My Life (1993)

Plot: Life is going well for Bob Jones, until he finds out that he is dying. He makes a videotape of his life for his unborn child, discovers things about himself, and comes to terms with his past.

Clip: A young boy prays/wishes upon a star for a circus to appear in his backyard (and then is crushed when no circus appears, to 4:15).

Time: (VHS) 1:50-2:28, length :38

Contact (1997)

Plot: Dr. Ellie Arroway (Jodie Foster), after years of searching, isolates a radio signal being transmitted from a distant planet. She and her fellow scientists decipher the transmission, and discover that it provides a blueprint for building a machine that allows her to contact the aliens.

Clip: The young Ellie sits up at night calling out to space through her ham radio. Scene segues to the adult Ellie, doing the same thing with big toys. This scene illustrates how some of us spend our whole lives keeping our eyes on the sky.

Time: (VHS) 7:01-7:53; (DVD) Chapter 2, 3:05-3:57; length :52

Awakenings (1990)

Plot: In 1969, a dedicated neurologist succeeds in bringing a middle-aged man out of a thirty-year catatonic state and learns something about life in the process. Based on a true story.

Clip: Dr. Sayer administers a large dose of an experimental medicine to one of the catatonic patients, Leonard, who miraculously wakes up from his coma. Begin the clip after the nurse says "good night," and end after Dr. Sayer says, "You're awake," and Leonard smiles.

Time: (VHS) 46:23-49:30, length 3:07

Clip: Having been awakened to life himself, Leonard urgently tells Dr. Sayer that "people need to be reminded of the joy of life" before they lose it. Clip begins with Dr. Sayer being awakened from sleep by the phone ringing, and ends after Leonard says, "the wonderment of life." (Alternate ending: after Dr. Sayer says, "We don't really know how to live" and opens the door; 01:25:13).

Time: (VHS) 1:22:24-1:24:55, length 2:31

Music

"Tower"—Cary Pierce. Contemporary alternative song, good for an opener or feature.

"Waiting for a Star to Fall"—Boy Meets Girl. Great '80s hit, but will require some lyric rewrites. Good for an opener.

"Come, Now is the Time to Worship"—Contemporary praise.

"O Come, O Come Emmanuel"—Advent hymn.

"Hail to the Lord's Anointed"—Christmas hymn.

"Lift Up Your Heads, You Mighty Gates"—Advent hymn.

Lumiclip Description

This short clip shows the perspective of someone staring up into the stars at night, trying to see a shooting star. The relaxing experience turns into surprise when the sky is reflected through the eye of the viewer.

Dramatic, mysterious. Running time :28.

Integration

Sermon Starters

The first Sunday of the new year (for lectionary users) focuses on the spirituality of paying attention, being awake, and watching for the coming of the Son of Man as the agent of God's new government in the world. "The Eye on the Sky" is a contemporary metaphor for the biblical experience of staying awake, waiting for the coming of the kingdom of God.

This passage comes from the section of Matthew often referred to as "the little apocalypse": Jesus' words about the last things of the age. It is sandwiched between the parable of the fig tree and the parable of the faithful and unfaithful servant, which both emphasize in figurative language the need to stay awake and pay attention for the Lord's return. This text uses the ancient metaphor of guards stationed on a watchtower or the wall of a city, who must be ever vigilant against the danger of falling asleep and allowing an enemy to attack.

Verse 36 addresses the persistent human tendency to speculate about the specific hour and day of his coming. Jesus reminds us that only God knows the time. The affirmation that nobody knows, not even the Son, is a clear injunction to let go of this desire to know exactly when the Son of Man will return.

The text compares the coming of the kingdom to the story of the flood. Only Noah and his family—by God's grace—were prepared for this cataclysmic event; everyone else perished. This is the analogy of the seriousness and scale of the coming of the Son of Man. Because the people in Noah's day refused to change their violent and sinful ways, to turn their hearts toward God, they were destroyed by God's wrath.

The metaphor of "being taken" and "being left" emphasizes the sharp division between those who pay attention and those who do not; between those who will be taken and saved, and those who will remain and perish in the destruction of the earth. These verses reflect the belief that those who believe will be plucked out of danger and saved from the last judgment and the destruction of the world. Those who do not will be left behind and destroyed.

The metaphor of the thief is another instance of emphasis on everyday experience as a framework for thinking about the coming of the Son of Man. In the ancient world, robbers often broke into houses under the cover of night. The word "broken into" literally means "dug through" and describes the actual way that thieves would dig through the sun-dried brick wall of ancient Palestinian houses. The metaphor addresses the frustration of people who were unable to stay awake to protect their homes, and therefore missed the time when the thief came.

These sayings focus on the need for perpetual readiness because we don't know the time of the coming of the Son of Man. The spirituality of Advent is the spirituality of paying attention, of waiting and watching for the birth of the Messiah.

Call to Worship

Have you ever lain outside at night, watching for shooting stars? Was it hard to stay awake? I remember doing that with friends. It seemed that every time I would doze off, they would "Ooh" and "Aah," having just caught sight of one. "Did you see that?!" Invariably, I missed out.

Watching for shooting stars was a job that required strict, patient attentiveness. In the Gospel of Matthew, Jesus tells us that waiting for God's coming is a lot like that. We don't know when exactly, but God is coming. Our job is to stay awake and keep our eye on the sky. Let's worship in a spirit of watching.

Prayer

Lord, help us stay awake. Give us hope that you are coming to heal the world. Show us the things in our lives that we don't see because our spirits are asleep. We want to be ready for your coming. Ready our hearts.

Closing Words/Benediction

As we go about our everyday activities, I invite you to remember that Jesus tells us to keep our eye on the sky. Stay attentive to the movement of God's spirit.

Drama

Perform a sketch about three people lying on lawn lounge chairs, staring up at the sky. One person keeps falling asleep, another repeatedly says, "I can't see anything," but the third catches sight of several shooting stars. End with a line such as, "Man, you don't want to miss these things! Keep your eye on the sky."

Display

Christmas decorations with a heavy emphasis on stars.

Surprise!

Overview

Stay awake for the coming guest of honor, Jesus.

Theme

Surprise!

Metaphor/Image

Surprise party

Treatment

In the parable of the absent householder, Jesus warns us of the necessity of staying awake and alert for the coming kingdom of God. This attitude of alert expectation comes from anticipation and excitement rather than from fear. It is like waiting at a surprise party for the guest of honor to arrive, so that the party may begin.

Human Need

We all want to be included in the "party," to be part of the people of God.

Experience

To capture the spiritual attitude of readiness, of staying awake for the coming of God's kingdom—the beginning of the party.

Word

Primary Scripture: Mark 13:(24-31), 32-37

Lectionary Week

First Sunday of Advent, Year B; Isaiah 64:1-9, Psalm 80:1-7, 17-19; 1 Corinthians 1:3-9

Related Scripture

Hebrews 2:1-4; 1 Samuel 24

Topics

Primary Topics

apocalypse, readiness, preparedness, kingdom of God, future, prophecy, celebration, Second Coming

Related Topics

authority, God's Word, belief, heaven

Movies

Mrs. Doubtfire (1993)

Plot: Daniel Hillard (Robin Williams), an unemployed, divorced actor, is unhappy about the time he gets to spend with his children. Daniel disguises himself as a nanny to get himself hired by his ex-wife Miranda (Sally Field).

Clip: In a classic example of being a party pooper, Miranda arrives home and puts an immediate stop to a rowdy party—complete with barnyard animals and kids jumping up and down on furniture—Daniel throws for his kids. In the middle of this scene, Miranda shouts, "What the hell is going on here?!", so you may want to use visuals only, or just use the first portion. As timed, the clip ends with Daniel saying, "Party's over."

Time: (VHS) 8:09-9:52, (DVD) Chapter 3, 00:37–2:20, length 1:43

Music

"Wake Up, Little Susy"—The Everly Brothers. Fun '50s song that is good for an opener.

"I Waited for the Lord on High"—Contemporary praise.

"I Stand in Awe"—Contemporary praise.

"Open Our Eyes"—Contemporary praise.

"Wake, Awake, for Night is Flying"—Hymn

Integration

Sermon Starters

The Gospel for this first day of the liturgical year—the beginning of the church year—occurs at the end of the apocalyptic discourse in Mark.

Using the contemporary metaphor of a surprise party, this worship experience points to the unexpected character of the kingdom of God. Just as one waits in excitement and anticipation for a surprise on one's birthday, so also one needs to be alert everyday for God's surprising presence.

In the Markan apocalypse, Jesus acts as the revealer of the future and the interpreter of the heavenly realm. The kingdom of God is a future realm or government that will come at God's initiative at some point in the future. This kingdom will be the fulfillment of God's promises. At its coming, the righteous will be rewarded and the wicked punished. While the kingdom of God may have been initiated with the ministry of Jesus, its coming in fullness is still in the future.

Jesus' apocalyptic discourse in Mark ends with the parable of the absent householder. In this parable, Jesus compares the coming of the kingdom of God with a man who goes on a journey, leaving his household in the charge of his servants until his return. This story invites listeners to identify with the servants, each of whom had distinct responsibilities and, in particular, with the doorkeeper, who was the principle guard of the house.

The parable focuses on the experience of the doorkeeper as he waits in anticipation for the coming of his master. The responsibility of the doorkeeper in ancient households was to open the door, which was kept locked, for anyone who wanted to enter, especially the master of the house. Because the doorkeeper does not know when the master will come back, the parable urges him to faithfully guard the door, staying alert for his master's return.

Jesus invites his listeners to identify with the doorkeeper's constant vigilance and readiness. Imagine trying to stay awake all the time in order to be ready to open the door. This is, of course, an exaggerated image. The Roman army, for example, divided the night into four watches of three hours each. A sentry or guard was then responsible for staying awake during those three hours. Jesus is not encouraging his listeners to never sleep.

This parable is about a spiritual attitude or posture of constant alertness and readiness. It is an advent parable that encourages us to foster a spirit of expectant waiting for the coming of God's kingdom.

Call to Worship

Start worship with the hushed anticipation of the impending arrival of the guest of honor at a surprise party. To create this atmosphere, the host might come up in character, grab the microphone, and say:

Listen up everybody! Okay, the guest of honor is about to arrive. We're going to practice. On the count of three, everyone yell 'Surprise!' Let's try that now.

Practice once or twice, then:

You [point to someone near the wall], watch that door. [Point to someone else] You watch that window. Get ready, and when [he/she] comes in, let's all yell, "Surprise!"

Out of character and as a "regular" worship leader:

[For lectionary users]: Today is the first Sunday of Advent, when we begin looking toward God's surprise for us—the birth of Jesus. Let's worship the God of surprises.

[For topical users]: Let's worship the God of surprises.

Prayer

Lord, we love you and your great surprise parties. You are truly the giver of the greatest gifts. Open our eyes and train our sensibilities to be aware of the signs of your presence with us. Make us alert. When we pray, help us to pay attention to the movement of your spirit within us. In all things, make us faithful servants, awake and ready for your coming. Amen.

Closing Words/Benediction

Go this week and get ready for God's party. Stay awake. Be ready, at any time, for the arrival of Jesus. Be ready to yell "Surprise!"

Display

Party items, balloons, streamers, hats, bowls of food, noise-makers, wrapped empty boxes, etc.

Other

Additional helps may be found in Tony Campolo's book, *The Kingdom of God is a Party.* (Nelson/Word Publishing Group, 1992). Consider serving cake after the service to continue the party theme.

EXPERIENCE THREE

Up All Night

Overview

Waiting for the Lord's coming.

Theme

Up All Night

Metaphor/Image

Watchtower

Treatment

Waiting for the Son of Man to arrive and the new age to come requires being alert and watchful for signs of his coming.

Human Need

When new and good things happen, we don't want to be the one who misses out because we're not paying attention.

Experience

A heightened sense of alertness to the signs of Jesus' coming in our lives; a wake-up call to pay attention.

Word

Primary Scripture: Luke 21:25-36

Lectionary Week

First Sunday of Advent, Year C; Jeremiah 33:114-16, Psalm 25:10, 1 Thessalonians 3:9-13

Related Scripture

Matthew 25:1-13, 1 Thessalonians 5:1-11

Topics

Primary Topics

apocalypse, signs, preparedness, readiness, kingdom of God, expectations

Related Topics

judgment, worry, depression, distraction

Music

"Wake-Up Call"—Phil Collins. '00s hit, for setting up the theme.

"Don't Want to Miss a Thing"—Aerosmith. '90's hit, for setting up the theme. For country fans, also covered by Mark Chesnutt.

"Wake, Awake for Night Is Flying"—hymn.

"My Lord, What a Morning"—hymn.

Lumiclip Description

An animated moment that captures the mystery and anxiety of waiting up at night for an expected visitor, as expressed through a lone, tall watchtower. Dramatic, reflective. Running Time: 0:25.

Integration

Sermon Starters

This is Luke's version of Jesus' apocalyptic discourse. Like guards in a watchtower, the community of the faithful is urged to stay awake. Another modern day equivalent familiar to many of us is the experience of staying up all night to prepare for an exam. The image of a lone, hilltop watchtower with light pouring out of its windows at night captures the dynamic of this experience.

The distinctive element in Luke's version of Jesus' apocalyptic discourse is the phrase "like a trap." Luke emphasizes that, for those who are unaware, the coming of the Son of Man can be like the sudden springing of a trap on unsuspecting animals or travelers. Jesus therefore urges his listeners to be aware, and to pray for strength to be able to "escape all these things that will take place."

Luke describes the coming of the new age using a number of apocalyptic metaphors. The signs and wonders in the heavens that will appear signal the cosmic transformation that will precede the coming of the Son of Man. Luke's account of this massive upheaval of creation redefines the nature of the conflict between good and evil in the world. The dominant framework for this worldly conflict, then and now, is built upon the identification of the enemy, represented by either a country or a group of people. The conflict between good and evil from this perspective then becomes a struggle between "us," the good guys, and "them," the enemy. The message of the New Testament redefines these apocalyptic symbols as it asserts a framework that sees everyone in the world as subject to the powers of evil. Only the intervention of God can free the world from domination by the powers of evil. This is the good news proclaimed by the coming of the kingdom of God.

Of course, what is good news for believers may be bad news for those who live their lives in drunkenness, dissipation, and worry about the things of this world. The coming of the kingdom of God will bring justice to the world and, therefore, punishment for the wicked as well as blessing for the righteous. In Luke's story, the coming of the Son of

Man is a symbol of hope for the future when God will decisively intervene in the world. In the context of God's decisive redemption of creation, the trials and tribulations that will be suffered during the judgment represent only the first step in making things right in the world. Staying alert, paying attention to the spiritual signs of the times, and praying steadily are all wise things to do during this season.

Jesus uses the image of the fig tree as another metaphor for staying alert to the signs of the coming of the kingdom of God. As both a beautiful tree and a source of delicious fruit, the fig tree was one of the most beloved trees of the land. Just as the first crocus and daffodils signal the arrival of spring for us, the first new leaves of the fig tree also announced the coming of spring. The spirituality associated with the fig tree is a spirit of joyful anticipation, of looking forward to the appearance of the first leaves and then rejoicing at the first signs of those new leaves. The fig tree thus represents a wonderful metaphor for a spirit of anticipation and watchfulness.

Jesus also recommends that we pray for the strength to stand through all the trials and tribulations of discipleship. For the people of the early church, this meant enduring persecution, mockery, and in some cases, death. For the church now, it may mean everything from dealing with the tension and exhaustion of sacrificial servant ministry to coping with rejection and criticism. Then, as now, we need God's help to steadily watch for the signs of God's kingdom.

Call to Worship

Are you a day person or a night person? Some of us have difficulty staying up late, while others have difficulty getting up early. When is the last time you stayed up all night?

May insert a personal story here.

In his warning of the signs of the end of the age, Jesus tells his disciples to be on guard and to be alert at all times for the coming of the Son of Man. Keeping watch is a twenty-four-hour-a-day job, and the commitment to stay awake is a challenge, regardless of our body rhythms. If we are to be ready for the Lord's coming, we need to be willing to be up all night.

Prayer

Lord, at the beginning of this new year of the Church, we pray that you would give us a spirit of watchfulness, a spirit of attention. Help us to show up, pay attention, and tell the truth in our prayers and in our lives during the year before us. We look for your coming in our midst. We want to pay attention to the signs of your presence among us. We look forward to what you will do in our future.

Closing Words/Benediction

The Lord be with you in your waking and your sleeping, in your watching and in your walking. The Lord give you strength to stand before the Son of Man when he comes. Wait and watch.

Drama

Two men in medieval gear keep watch in a tower. The first (straight) man is alert and talkative, while the second man is dying of fatigue as he vainly tries to stay awake. Funny moments could include the second man agreeing to ridiculous stuff or talking nonsense (think Monty Python).

Display

Alarm clocks, time clocks, coffee pots, lamps, radios, staying up accoutrements.

God's Coming
and
You're Going to Get It

Overview

God is love, not judgment.

Theme

God's Coming and You're Going to Get It

Metaphor/Image

'50s serial movie look; horror parody

Treatment

Many people view God primarily as a harsh judge who, like a '50s disaster movie monster, wreaks havoc on wrong-doers. This experience emphasizes God's love rather than God's judgment.

Human Need

We are gripped by the power of fear and shame, and we need to know God cares about us.

Experience

To experience God as love and not judgment.

Word

Primary Scripture: Matthew 3:1-12

Lectionary Week

Second Week of Advent, Year A; Isaiah 11:1-10, Psalm 72:1-7, 18-19, Romans 15:4-13

Related Scripture

1 John 4, John 3:16-17, Luke 3:15-17, 21-22

Topics

Primary Topics

judgment, misconceptions, love, baptism

Related Topics

fear, hatred, grace, law, clean, unclean

Movies

The Blob (1988)

Plot: A strange gelatinous organism crashes into a small town and begins eating everything in its path.

Clip: The blob attacks the city and a priest reacts by saying, "It has been prophesied."

Time: (VHS) 1:21:21-1:21:48, length :27

Independence Day (1996)

Plot: Aliens invade earth and destroy most of its major cities, throwing the world into panic. A small group manages to defeat invaders and preserve freedom from total invasion.

Clip: There is madness on the streets as David Levinson (Jeff Goldblum) and his father make plans to run away.

Time: (VHS) 30:54, (DVD) Chapter 14 0:00-0:28, time :28

Music

"It's the End of the World as We Know It"—REM. This '80s hit makes a good opener.

"I Could Sing of Your Love Forever"—Contemporary praise

"Trading My Sorrows"—Contemporary praise

"Come Just as You Are"—Contemporary praise

"O Come, O Come Emmanuel"—Christmas hymn

"Prepare Ye the Way of the Lord"—from the *Godspell* soundtrack. This show tune is good for an opener or feature.

Integration

Sermon Starters

The story of John the Baptist emphasizes the need to pay attention to the coming kingdom of God. Sometimes John and Jesus talk about the kingdom as a new age that has already begun, but usually it is described as a new time *about* to arrive. John calls for "repentance"—which literally means "turnaround"—in preparation for God's coming. This is the spirituality of Advent, the time of watching, waiting, and preparing for the coming of Christ.

The quotation from Isaiah identifies John as the one who comes to prepare the way, who proclaims God's coming decisively to intervene in history. The description of John's clothing and food also identifies him as Elijah (2 Kings 1:8), the one who precedes the coming of the Messiah (Malachi 4:5).

In verses 7-10, John reacts sharply to the Pharisees and Sadducees who had come to be baptized, comparing them to a "brood of vipers." In the Bible the snake is the most conniving of creatures and the viper is the most poisonous. The meaning of these words about the Pharisees and Sadducees is that highly religious people cannot claim their religiosity as the basis for not being judged in the coming age of the Messiah. Likewise, being Jewish and a "child of Abraham" (or a member of any other ethnic or racial group) counts for nothing. The only thing that counts is righteousness that grows out of true repentance. The wrath to come refers to "the imminent judgment of God."

Although John baptizes with water, Jesus will baptize with the Holy Spirit and with fire. These images allude to both dimensions of the coming of the kingdom of God: the blessings of the Holy Spirit and the judgment and potential punishment associated with the fire of hell and the last judgment. Fire, like water, is a purifying element and may refer to the Holy Spirit as an agent of purification.

The author assumes that his listeners know the process of threshing grain. The winnowing fork or shovel was used to throw the grain into the air so that the wind could blow away the chaff, the loose covering surrounding the grain. Clearing the threshing floor meant cleaning the threshing floor of all the fallen chaff. The grain was stored for future use while the chaff was gathered into a pile and burned. Likewise, at the coming judgment, the unfaithful will be separated from the faithful and consumed.

This is a thoroughly Jewish story with lots of exaggerated language, vivid metaphors, and high emotion. Designed to get the listener's attention, this story reverses the expectation that the coming of the kingdom will be a time of blessing, insisting instead that it will be a time of judgment. Today this association of the coming of the kingdom of God with judgment and disaster has not only become common, but is, in fact, the dominant one in contemporary culture. However, underneath the stern warnings about coming judgment lies the absolute conviction that God is in control, that God is working in history to restore creation, and that God will set us free from the powers of evil. But a pivotal step in God's work is our own self-examination and repentance. The good news is that God hears our confessions and gathers us into God's granary.

Call to Worship

Communicate the theme of anticipating judgment, but instead finding grace. An example: Ask people if they have ever had the experience of tensing up in expectation of being yelled at or struck, but instead received a compliment or a soft touch.

Or, show the scene from *Independence Day*, followed by:

"Like Jeff Goldblum, we want to make plans to run away from the destruction. We want to run from the wrath of God when we think that God's coming into our lives. But the arrival of God is something completely different..."

Prayer

Lord, God of heaven and earth, forgive us for our sins. Blot out our transgressions and take not your Holy Spirit from us. If you were to judge us according to your laws, you would be justified in casting us out of your presence.

Yet you surround us with love and forgiveness. The great surprise of your coming into our lives is your spirit of grace. Give us confidence in your spirit and the freedom to live without fear.

Closing Words/Benediction

God is love. Not a weak love, but a strong, complete love. Go and see the love of God in your life this week.

Display

Old film reels and film projectors.

Trailblazer

Overview

Clearing the wilderness and preparing for Jesus' coming

Theme

Trailblazer

Metaphor/Image

Lone scout

Treatment

Like a lone scout who blazes a trail and shows people the safe way to go, John the Baptist prepared people for Christ's coming by calling them to repentance and baptism. We too are called to repentance.

Human Need

We all must navigate wildernesses, and we all need a trailblazer who knows what is ahead and can guide us. We want to feel prepared for what is to come.

Experience

To respond to the call for repentance, as did the first hearers of John's call in Mark's Gospel

Word

Primary Scripture: Mark 1:1-8

Lectionary Week

Second Week of Advent, Year B; Isaiah 40:1-11, Psalm 85:1-2, 8-13, 2 Peter 3:8-15

Related Scripture

Luke 3:1-20, John 1:6, 15, 19-28, Acts 13:24-25

Topics

Primary Topics

baptism, Advent, anticipation, sin, repentance

Related Topics

mission, calling, preparedness

Movies

Dances with Wolves (1990)

Plot: Lt. John Dunbar (Kevin Costner), assigned to a remote Civil War outpost in the Dakotas territory, arrives to discover it abandoned. In his exile there, he befriends a wolf, and allies himself with a local Sioux tribe. As the army reaches Sioux territory, Dunbar must choose between his allegiance to the military and his allegiance to the Sioux.

Clip: When the buffalo return in a nighttime stampede, Dunbar tells the tribe of the good news. His narration recounts how the Indian scouts find the trail, just as he had said. This clip provides a good metaphor for the news proclaimed by John the Baptist. Since this clip is rather long, you may want to shorten it.

Time: (VHS) 1:17:01-1:21:20. (DVD) Chapter 12, 0:00-4:19, length 4:19

O Brother, Where Art Thou? (2000)

Plot: Based loosely on Homer's *Odyssey*, this movie follows the adventures of three escaped convicts—Everett Ulysses McGill (George Clooney) and his companions Delmar and Pete—on their quest to reach Everett's home and recover the hidden loot from their bank robbery.

Clip: The trio is surprised by the arrival of a large crowd of people headed to the river for baptism. One of them runs to join in the ceremony, followed by another. Watch for language at 19:12 and 19:27.

Time: (VHS) 17:48-20:12, (DVD) Chapter 4, 2:40-5:04, length 2:24

The Apostle (1998)

Plot: A country preacher named Sonny (Robert Duvall) has a transforming spiritual experience after committing a brutal crime.

Clip: To redeem himself after his crime of passion, Sonny baptizes himself in the river, renaming himself the Apostle E.F.

Time: (VHS) 43:33-44:16, (DVD) Chapter 14, 0:00-:43, length :43

Music

"Prepare Ye the Way of the Lord"—from the *Godspell* soundtrack; use as an opener.

"Happy Trails"—Roy Rogers and Dale Evans. Good to close worship.

"Daniel Boone"—Disney song; fun for an opener.

"God Will Make a Way"—Classic "contemporary" praise.

"Cleanse Me"—Contemporary praise.

"Prepare the Way of the Lord"—Taizé chant.

"Lead Me Lord"—hymn.

Integration

Sermon Starters

Mark's Gospel begins by introducing John the Baptist, God's messenger, who proclaims the coming of the Anointed One of God. According to the prophecy in Isaiah, John goes before the Lord, preparing his way, making his "paths straight," blazing his trail. Unquestionably a historical figure, John stood in the tradition of the prophets who proclaimed the imminent judgment of God against Israel. His distinctiveness was that he developed the ritual of baptism as a concrete sign of both a new commitment to a pure and sinless life and God's forgiveness of all of the sins of the past.

John's appearance is presented as the fulfillment of prophecy. The prophecy was that the Messiah, the Mighty One, would have a forerunner who would prepare the way for the Messiah. Thus, Malachi 4:5-6 reads: "Lo, I will send you the prophet Elijah before the great and terrible day of the Lord comes. He will turn the hearts of parents to their children and the hearts of children to their parents, so that I will not come and strike the land with a curse." The actual quotation in Mark is a composite of Malachi 3:1 (Mk. 1:2b) and Isaiah 40:3 (Mk. 1:3). This merging probably reflects the processes of oral memory and recitation of the Scriptures either in Mark's mind or in the traditions of the community.

The description of John draws unmistakable reference to Elijah. In 2 Kings 1:8, Elijah is described as "a hairy man, with a leather belt around his waist." His diet of locusts and wild honey was the food of the wilderness. According to wilderness aficionados, locusts roasted over a fire have a crunchy texture and a nutty flavor; wild honey could be found in beehives in trees or sometimes among the rocks. The expectation, based on the Malachi prophecy, was that Elijah would return to lead the way for the Messiah.

The baptism of John was a "baptism of repentance for the forgiveness of sins." This phrase meant that persons were baptized as a sign both of their repentance from past sins and of the forgiveness of those sins. John's baptism was in contrast to the purification baths that were a regular practice in Judaism. For example, every month after their period women would take a ritual purification bath as part of their cleansing. Likewise men would take a ritual bath after a nocturnal emission. D.E. Nineham gives a clear description of the character of John's baptism:

> "What he promised was that, if men would truly repent of their sins, his cleansing of their bodies in water might be an effective sign of the cleansing of their souls from guilt, so that they could become members of the New Israel, cleansed and ready for the coming judgment...he merely faced people with the choice: 'Either my water baptism now for forgiveness, or, very soon, the Messiah's fire-baptism—i.e. the painful prospect of (condemning) judgment.'"(60-61)

The fact that all of the people go out to John is not to be taken literally, but rather is Mark's way of saying that the whole nation repented as a preparation for the coming of the great and terrible day of the Lord. National repentance was required as preparation for the coming of the Messiah.

The story of John the Baptist generates energy and anticipation about the coming of the Messiah. John proclaims that the centuries Israel has waited for redemption by the coming Messiah are now reaching fulfillment. Like a bride and groom who have looked forward to the fulfillment of their desire, Israel looked forward to the fulfillment of God's promises and to the redemption of all of creation that the Messiah would bring. The focus of the fulfillment of this yearning is on the act of repentance. The gift of baptism inaugurates one personally into the new kingdom. And it is at some level a gift for each individual who is baptized.

For United Methodists, the circuit rider is an image of the trailblazer who continued John the Baptist's spirit. The circuit riders lived in the wilderness and brought God's message by riding through dangerous territory. They were a living metaphor of the coming of God's messenger for the people who lived in the American wilderness.

Call to Worship

We forget that the cities we live in were once empty fields or forests, and that someone had to cut through the thickets and brush to carve out paths that became roads and eventually highways. We call those people trailblazers.

Today we celebrate the life of a trailblazer of God's spirit. John the Baptist came to clear a path for the coming of Christ, and we still experience the effects of his prophetic mission. Let's worship the God who sends trailblazers to prepare our way.

Storytelling/Scripture Recital

This story may be told in the style of a Western, so the storyteller might wear a Stetson and jeans or overcoat and tell the story in the style of an old campfire ballad, with lonely guitar music in the background (á la Jim Reeves). You may also try a Western accent.

Prayer

Lead the congregation in a prayer of confession and repentance to prepare them for the coming of the Lord. The pastor could take on the role of John the Baptist, calling people to repentance, to which the congregation responds with a litany, "Forgive us, Lord." The pastor's lines might include:

> Leader: "For those things that we did that we ought not have done"
>
> **Congregation: "Forgive us, Lord."**
>
> Leader: "For those things we didn't do but we should have done"
>
> **Congregation: "Forgive us, Lord."**
>
> Leader: "For our sins as a nation"
>
> **Congregation: "Forgive us, Lord."**
>
> Leader: "For our indifference to the signs of your coming"
>
> **Congregation: "Forgive us, Lord."**

Closing Words/Benediction

Go in the peace and the love of a Lord who comes to us in the wilderness, who sends trailblazers to clear the obstructions that prevent us from meeting God on the path.

Drama

Lead a "faith walk". One person who can see leads a number of blindfolded people by calling out a series of directions like "step up," "turn right," etc.

Display

Chaps, saddlebag, sleeping bag, walking stick, and even a rough path marked by stones and/or dirt (on a tarp!).

Earth Movers

Overview

When we serve those in need, we help prepare the way for the Lord.

Theme

Earth Movers

Metaphor/Image

Bulldozer clearing a path

Treatment

As followers of Jesus, we are called to stand in the shoes of John the Baptist and prepare the way for the Messiah through humble acts of discipleship, service, and witness to others. The synergy of our small, individual acts as "Christ preparers" has the power to move the earth.

Human Need

As evidenced in the days following the World Trade Center tragedy, most people want to do something constructive, to be a part of something bigger than themselves. They need direction and a purpose for their desire to do something concrete and specific.

Experience

Like his words about John the Baptist, Jesus praises those who prepare others for him. This experience will inspire people to serve and humbly subordinate their own glory for the sake of the Kingdom of God.

Word

Primary Scripture: Matthew 11:2-11

Lectionary Week

Third week of Advent, Year A; Isaiah 35:1-10, Psalm 146:5-10, James 5:7-10

Related Scripture

Matthew 25:31-46, Isaiah 61:1-4, Luke 4:18-19, Romans 12:9-21

Topics

Primary Topics

humility, service, preparation, Messiah, prophecy, prophet

Related Topics

Advent, evangelism

Movies

Pay it Forward (2000)

Plot: A young boy's teacher challenges his class to do something that will change the world. The boy decides to do three good things for someone who, in turn, will do something good for three other people; thus repaying each kindness forward, rather than back.

Clip: A sixth grade teacher challenges his students to do something that will change the world. The clip begins with "this year's assignment…" and ends with, "squeak by with a C."

Time: (VHS) 10:09-11:50, (DVD) Chapter 3, 2:34-4:15, length 1:41

Sister Act (1992)

Plot: Deloris Van Carter (Whoopi Goldberg), a lounge singer in Vegas, witnesses her mobster boyfriend murder someone and is placed in protective custody in a convent. She transforms the choir.

Clip: The convent reaches out to the neighborhood to help people. This clip is a musical montage that could work with music or without (underneath something else, for example).

Time: (VHS) 1:00:05-1:03:10, length 3:05

Music

"I Feel the Earth Move Under My Feet"—Carole King. '70s hit, great for an opener.

"Change the World"—Eric Clapton. Great for a feature.

"Man in the Mirror"—Michael Jackson. Good for a feature.

"We Can a Make a Difference"—Jaci Valesquez. '90s Contemporary Christian hit. Great for a closer.

"Go Forth for God"—hymn.

"Jesu, Jesu"—hymn.

"Prepare Ye the Way of the Lord"—from the *Godspell* soundtrack. Show tune, good for an opener or a feature.

Lumiclip Description

An earth-shaking, heavy-metal look at the large vehicles that move huge amounts of dirt. Hard-driving, edgy. Running time: 30.

Integration

Sermon Starters

This passage raises the central question of Jesus' identity. John raises the question that everyone had been wondering: "Are you the one who is to come, or are we to wait for another?" Is the Messiah this man who heals physical affliction, who gives new life to the dead, who brings hope and good news to the poor? Why did John ask this question? Did he have doubts? After all, in Matthew 3:11ff, John describes the Messiah as the powerful One who would come to carry out God's judgment, which was entirely in line with popular belief. Matthew implies that John simply didn't know Jesus. Though Luke 1 implies that John and Jesus not only knew each other but were also related, Matthew doesn't say anything about this. Having heard about the deeds of Jesus from his prison cell, John suspects that Jesus is the Messiah and wants to get confirmation.

Jesus is clearly identified as the Messiah, but not the kind of Messiah many expected. Rather than bringing fiery judgment, Jesus brings healing and wholeness, life and hope. The specific deeds Jesus performs—giving sight to the blind, making the lame walk, and restoring hearing to the deaf—all echo descriptions of the Messiah found in Isaiah 35:5-6; 42:18; and 61:1. Significant differences are: 1) in Isaiah, the coming of the new age is also accompanied by the punishment of God's enemies, while Jesus here speaks only of deliverance; 2) the Isaiah passages do not include the cleansing of lepers or the resurrection of the dead; 3) the good news to the poor is an entirely new element. These differences are signs of Matthew's understanding of the kingdom of God. The signs of the

Messianic Kingdom of Jesus are signs of freedom from domination by the powers of evil.

The last statement of blessing for the one who does not take offense is difficult to translate with sufficient force. The Greek word, "to be scandalized, offended" (*skandali-zo*) refers to the everyday experience of walking in sandals on rocky roads and stubbing one's toe on a rock. The anger at and cursing of the stone that follows such a stubbing is what this word refers to. Many in Israel were scandalized by this definition of Messiahship and the kingdom of God. And there are also many people today who are put off by such a definition. Many of us want immediate political, economic, and military solutions to the powers of evil.

The text then turns to the question of John's identity. Jesus identifies him as a prophet, as the one foretold who would "prepare the way" for the Messiah. Jesus asks the crowd why they went out to see John. John was wildly popular, and crowds from all over Judea went to listen to him. Jesus' rhetorical questions probe his listeners' motives and expectations and the answer to both inquiries is "No": they didn't go out to see the tall canegrass along the Jordan River being blown by the wind, nor did they go out to see someone dressed in fine clothes. They went out to see a prophet.

Jesus affirms John as being both a prophet and greater than a prophet. The source of John's stature is his humility and utter commitment to the kingdom of God. John embodies the spirit of willingness to subordinate one's own glory for the sake of the Messiah. The concluding statement about the least in the kingdom of God is an affirmation of the extraordinary benefit and privilege present for Jesus' followers in their participation in the government of God that Jesus brings.

John models discipleship for us. Whoever prepares the way for the coming of the Messiah as the agent of the government of God follows in John's footsteps. Isaiah's metaphor refers to this forerunner as one who "makes the rough places plain and the crooked places straight." The prophet of God's new age creates a straight and level road through the wilderness and is an earth mover who lets nothing stand in the way of the coming of God's Messiah.

This story invites us to tell the stories of people in our congregation and in the wider community who have embodied this role. Mahatma Gandhi is one example, preparing the way for an independent India and for other leaders who followed him.

Call to Worship

Adapt as needed.

I was driving down the highway the other day when I saw several new roads being built. Particularly as I passed through hilly terrain, I noticed in many areas that the curved places were being straightened and the mountains were being flattened. Preparing those roads is an enormous job that takes years and requires the work of huge earth movers.

Just like those highway builders, we have a job to do. We also must work to prepare the Way of the Lord. God's prophets such as John the Baptist called people to become "earth movers," preparing the way for Christ's coming. Let's hear that call today as we worship together.

Prayer

How do we move the earth? It sounds like such an enormous job.

But in actuality, we do it one scoop at a time. Hear these words of Jesus (from Matthew 11:5): "Go and tell John what you hear and see: the blind receive their sight, the lame walk, the lepers are cleansed, the deaf hear, the dead are raised, and the poor have good news brought to them."

Ask God to show you ways that you can move the earth this week. As you are led, offer these up to God in prayer, and to each we will respond: "Lord, help us prepare your Way."

Closing Words/Benediction

Go and be "earth movers" this coming week. Find ways to serve others in humility. Serve food at a shelter. Take gifts to those in need. [If part of Advent] Invite people to come next week for Christmas Eve worship. Find ways to be a path maker for Jesus. All of those little actions, together, will change the world.

Display

Toy bulldozers, little scoops of the earth (dirt, rocks, stones).

Do the Right Thing

Overview

Discerning the right thing to do in difficult situations

Theme

Do the Right Thing

Metaphor/Image

Close-up of Joseph and Mary with baby

Treatment

This is the Christmas story from Joseph's point of view. Faced with a difficult situation, Joseph wanted to make the right decision, but first he had to figure out exactly what that was among apparently competing values.

Human Need

Most people want to do the right thing, but often find themselves in difficult situations, struggling to figure out what they should do.

Experience

Doing the right thing means listening carefully to God and following God's will first.

Word

Primary Scripture: Matthew 1:18-25

Lectionary Week

Fourth Sunday of Advent, Year A; Isaiah 7:10-16, Psalm 80:11-7, 17-19, Romans 1:1-7

Related Scripture

Genesis 22:1-19, Acts 8:1-48, Acts 15:1-35

Topics

Primary Topics

discernment, obedience, trust, faith

Related Topics

prayer, decision-making, consulting, Bible, accountability, society, norms

Movies

Remember the Titans (2000)

Plot: Chronicles the true story of a newly appointed African-American coach (Denzel Washington) and high school team on their first season as a racially integrated unit.

Clip: Football star Gary Bertier (Ryan Hurst) is forced to choose between hanging out with his white school friends or with his mixed-race teammates. The clip requires setup, but it is a good illustration of maintaining commitment in the face of pressure.

Time: (VHS) 51:59-53:18, (DVD) Chapter 16, 2:334-3:53, length 1:19

Field of Dreams (1989)

Plot: Iowa corn farmer Ray Kinsella (Kevin Costner) hears voices that lead him to build a baseball diamond in his cornfield. He and his family are then visited by the Chicago Black Sox.

Clip: With his brother-in-law on one side with papers to sell the farm, and Terrence Mann (James Earl Jones) on the other side saying people will come, Ray must decide whether or not to see his crazy dream through. Good example of perseverance suitable for use as a sermon clip related to the theme. The entire scene begins at 1:20:46, but the times indicated below are of Ray's big decision. Another option is to cut the last 10 seconds and not show Ray's decision.

Time: (VHS) 1:23:15-1:26:05, length 2:50

Music

"I Got My Mind Set on You"—George Harrison. This '80s song makes a good opener. Requires minor lyric rewrites.

"Hark the Herald Angels Sing"—Christmas hymn.

"Emmanuel"—Christmas song.

"Praise the Name of Jesus"—Contemporary praise.

Integration

Sermon Starters

The first story in Matthew's Gospel (after the genealogy) focuses on Jesus' father and his character as he struggles with how to respond to Mary's pregnancy. Mary had become pregnant during their engagement even though they had not had sexual intercourse. In the story, Matthew explains to the audience that she is pregnant by the Holy Spirit.

At first, Joseph decides to choose the most compassionate option available to him. According to the letter of the law, he could have had Mary tried before a public court. If she was found guilty of adultery—the only reasonable explanation for her pregnancy—she could have been executed by stoning. Even if she had been allowed to live, Mary would have been publicly humiliated and condemned to a life of shame as the mother of an illegitimate child.

Instead, Joseph resolves to divorce her quietly without a public trial. The narrator assumes that everyone in his audience knows the implications of the situation and will judge Joseph's decision to be both righteous and compassionate.

One dimension of this story worth noting is the "inside" knowledge the audience has about the pregnancy. They know the true source of Mary's pregnancy, and from that perspective, Joseph's decision to send her away is clearly wrong. The story implies that if Joseph knew how Mary had gotten pregnant, he would embrace her rather than divorce her. But how can he find out since Mary is apparently unwilling to risk telling him? Perhaps she too was uncertain about what has happened.

Most of the story describes the appearance of a messenger from God to Joseph in a dream. As listeners, we are inside Joseph's mind as he sleeps, experiencing his dream with him. The messenger tells Joseph what the audience already knows.

Not only does the messenger reveal to Joseph that Mary's pregnancy is an act of God, but he also tells him what to name the baby. *Jesus* is the Greek name related to the Hebrew name, *Joshua*. It roughly means, "God saves" or "God delivers." The angel's explanation of the name draws out this implication, "for he will save his people from their sins."

This deeper look at the meaning behind the name of Jesus is typical of the ritual of naming in Hebrew storytelling. For example, the name "Isaac" (Gen. 21:5) linguistically relates to the word for "laugh" and is connected with his mother's laughter when the angels tell Abraham he will have a son (Gen. 18) as well as the joyous laughter of Sarah's friends (Gen. 21:6).

This story of divine counseling for expectant fathers also relates to the stories of Abraham and God's promise that he would have a son (Gen. 15:1-6: "Do not be afraid, Abram;" Gen.17:15-21: "your wife Sarah shall bear you a son, and you shall name him Isaac.") Stories of irregular births are some of the favorite stories of God's activity in the narrative traditions of Israel.

The narrator concludes the story of the dream with an explicit narrative comment to the audience explaining that this dream, and indeed this whole event, is the fulfillment of Isaiah's prophecy. The second name for the child, "Emmanuel," plays no further role in the story but is fully appropriate as a description of what Jesus does: he acts in ways that embody the spirit of God.

The final episode of the story describes Joseph's new course of action. He does what the angel instructs and takes Mary as his wife. The listeners know what this meant for Joseph. None of his family or friends would believe either Mary's story or his. In contrast to the story of Abraham and Sarah, this irregular birth was not a source of laughter and good cheer for Jesus' parents. Questions about the legitimacy of their child have been raised from then until now. Though Matthew's story has continued to be the dominant explanation and an ongoing source of wonder, questions still remain.

Through this story the audience shares Joseph's internal discernment of the spirit of God in the conception, birth, and naming of his son. It is an intimate experience of how discernment of God's presence in the events of human life can change our way of acting and our way of being. As listeners, we experience Joseph as a truly righteous and holy man, a man who did the right thing. It is also a story about the intimate relationship between God and human beings. This story about Joseph and Mary depicts a God who acts in history and individual lives—in the conception of the child, the dream, the name, and the fulfillment of the Scripture.

The story invites us to identify with and tell the stories of people who struggle to discern and do the right thing when it would inevitably be misunderstood.

Call to Worship

Start with a telling of the Matthew 1 story.

Joseph was in deep trouble. He was faced with a difficult situation, with no easy answers, and he had to figure out what to do. Has anyone here ever been in a situation like this?

We'd all like to have an angel tell us the right thing to do. It would be so much easier than having to struggle to make the right decision. Though an angel did appear to Joseph in a dream, he probably also struggled as well. It is more likely, that as a 'righteous man,' he discerned God's will the way followers have always discerned God's will, and continue to do so today. Let's spend some time in Joseph's story, and maybe learn a bit about how to hear our own angels.

Storytelling/Scripture Recital

Try to create an atmosphere where people may experience Joseph's struggle, though the listeners already know the story and how Mary came to be with child. One way to do this would be to change the tone from an objective observer in verse 18 to a tone of engagement, involvement, stress, and tension in the description of Joseph. The words of the angel, then, become consolation to him in his agony.

Prayer

Lord, when we don't know what to do and are trying to discern the right thing, help us remember Joseph's agony as the father of the Christ child. Although he didn't know what to do, Joseph trusted you in the end. We pray that we also might hear your voice to guide us in our own struggles.

Invite people to pray silently for their own struggles.

In this Christmas season, when our tensions and uncertainties are often magnified, give us the confidence and the trust to ask you to be ever present with us. Amen.

Closing Words/Benediction

May the spirit of God grant you both the discernment and the ability to do the right thing. And may the blessing of God—Father, Son, and Holy Spirit—be with you and empower you in every good thing, both to know and fulfill God's purpose for your life, now and forevermore.

Display

Create a display using a baby blanket and various other things that communicate Christmas as it relates to the biblical story.

Let It Be

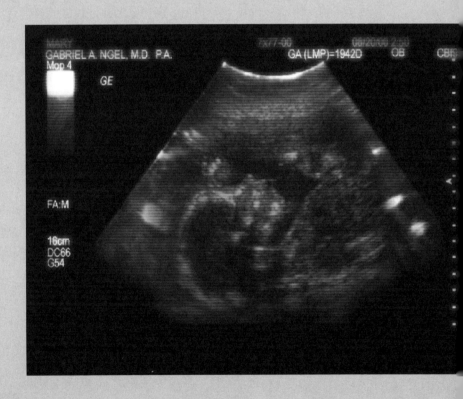

Overview

Learning to live so that we are open to God's possibilities rather than trying to control every aspect of our lives

Theme

Let It Be

Metaphor/Image

Sonogram

Treatment

We are often faced with decisions that seem impossible and mandates that don't make sense. Mary responds to the angel's announcement that she will bear the Son of God with complete openness and willingness: "Here I am, the servant of the Lord; let it be with me according to your word." Mary's humble obedience and acceptance of this awesome task serves as an inspiration for us to live life open to possibility rather than closed to anything other than our own needs and desires.

Human Need

We all fear the inability to control our own lives and need courage to accept God's will for our lives.

Experience

That we experience a loving God who calls us to live a life surrendered to God's control, and to decide to live in accordance with God's agenda

Word

Primary Scripture: Luke 1:26-38

Lectionary Week

Fourth Week of Advent, Year B; 2 Samuel 7:1-11, 16, Psalm 89:1-4, 19-26, Romans 16:25-27

Related Scripture

Genesis 18:1-15, 1 Samuel 3:2-9, Luke 1:8-20

Topics

Primary Topics

life of Jesus, faith, God's will, God's plan, choice, surrender, decision, calling, destiny, courage, humility, servanthood

Related Topics

Mother's Day, gender, sexuality

Movies

Where the Heart Is (2000)

Plot: Novalee Nation (Natalie Portman), pregnant seventeen-year-old, is abandoned by her boyfriend at a Wal-Mart in rural Oklahoma as they head toward California. With no money and no place to stay, Novalee hides in the Wal-Mart, eating canned food and sleeping on a lawn chair, until her baby is born. With the help of strangers, Novalee stays in this small Oklahoma town and makes a life for herself and her daughter.

Clip: After birthing a baby in a Wal-Mart, Novalee expresses fear about her future, until the nurse brings her new baby. This clip provides a good example of letting go of fear and simply living.

Time: (VHS) 28:01-29:50, (DVD) Chapter 7, 0:00-1:49, length 1:49

Music

"Let It Be"—The Beatles. A huge hit with appropriate lyrics, great for an opener.

"Sweet Child O' Mine"—Guns 'N Roses song, covered by Sheryl Crow. Top forty hit, good for an opener.

"(What if God Was) One of Us"—Joan Osborne. Top forty hit.

"With Arms Wide Open"—Creed. A top forty song dedicated to the singer's newborn daughter. Heartbeat noises open and close the song. Good for an opener or feature.

"What Child Is This"—Christmas hymn.

"Let All Mortal Flesh Keep Silence"—Traditional hymn.

Lumiclip Description

This video clip uses the image of a sonogram to create a moving visual interpretation of the story of the angel appearing to the young woman Mary, as told in the Gospel of Luke. This Lumiclip may be used with the storyteller's voice as a complete clip, or without the storyteller's voice as a background for a live telling of the story. Contemplative, inspirational. Running time 1:03.

Integration

Sermon Starters

This passage, referred to as the "Annunciation," tells the intimate story of Gabriel's announcement to Mary that she would become the mother of the Messiah. Although Gabriel does most of the speaking and acting in the story, we as listeners hear his words from Mary's point of view. The climax of the story is Mary's affirmation and acceptance of the vocation to which she has been called by God: "Let it be with me according to your word."

Mary's words have often been interpreted as her passive agreement with the Lord's plans for her. But the birth announcement stories in the Old Testament follow the pattern of depicting women who have earnestly and aggressively sought a child. These women, in whose lineage Mary stands, are not passive receivers, but are fully active participants in God's saving activity. It is more likely that Mary's final words to the angel were a strong affirmation and acceptance of God's election of her rather than a passive resignation to God's strong will.

The story of John's conception provides the frame for the announcement about Jesus, since it both precedes (1:5-25) and follows (1:39-56) the annunciation story. In fact, the announcement of Jesus' birth directly parallels the announcement of John's birth. Thus, Luke 1-2 is structured by this connection:

Announcements concerning John (1:5-25) and Jesus (1:26-38)
The meeting of Mary and Elizabeth (1:39-56)
Birth, circumcision, prophecy, and childhood of John (1:57-80) and of Jesus (2:1-52)

These stories in turn echo the announcement and birth of Ishmael and Isaac (Genesis 15:1-6; 16:1-16; 18:1-15; 21:1-20), of Samson (Judges 13), and of Samuel (I Sam. 1-2:10). In contrast to Matthew, Luke uses this Old Testament pattern in his story of Jesus' birth. The elements of the narrative pattern that are variously present in these particular stories are: the entrance of an angel or of God; the perplexity of the hearer; the heavenly message; the objection; the reassurance and sign; the birth; and the glorification of the Lord. When seen and heard in the context of this narrative tradition, the impact of these stories is even greater. John's birth required the miracle of an old woman conceiving a child, as had the conception of Isaac. The mothers of Samson and Samuel received the miracle of conceiving a child though they had previously been barren. But the birth of Jesus required an even greater miracle: the conception of a child by a virgin. Although God's intervention was present in all of these instances, the story of Jesus' birth represents the culmination of the tradition.

The story clarifies Jesus' identity and role. Thus, the two parts of the angel's message are 1) that he will be the Davidic Messiah (1:31-33) and 2) that he will be the Son of God (1:35). Although Jesus is identified as the Son of God in all the Gospels, each presents a different and evolving picture of when he became Son of God. In early stages of the community, Jesus was affirmed as Messiah and Son of God in the aftermath of his resurrection with the implication that he became God's Son then (Acts 2:36). In Mark, Jesus becomes God's son at his baptism. In Luke, Jesus is identified as God's Son at his birth. And John identifies Jesus' identity as Son of God at the beginning of time. One can see the development of early Christian stories about Jesus' identity in this evolving narrative tradition.

Furthermore, this story has had a strong and energetic life in the history of Christian tradition. The glorification of Mary and the development of the extensive oral and doctrinal traditions about Mary has been one of the major motifs in the history of Christian thought. Mary is presented as "the favored one" who is the model of Christian discipleship and the handmaiden of the Lord. She fully cooperates with God's plan of salvation.

Luke focuses on the experience of Mary in this story. What was it like for a fifteen-year-old (or even younger) woman to receive such a message from God? What were the social consequences for her of being pregnant before she was married? Most important, how did she understand what God was doing? Obviously, she couldn't fully understand what God was doing. She could only trust that God would make something of this highly unusual situation. We can see in retrospect that her faith in God was fully appropriate.

This story reveals a dynamic that is present in the life of every person. We learn to accept and affirm God's will and purpose in trust. We do so without knowing where it will lead or what God will be able to do in the future. This gets at the heart of Advent. Advent is waiting in anticipation of God's coming. This waiting involves learning to trust God. The recognition of the traditions of God's involvement in the conception and birth of the religious leaders of Israel is both a source of wonder in itself and a sign of God's involvement in the lives of each person. We don't know what God will make of us. We too can learn to say with Mary, "Let it be with me according to your word."

Call to Worship

How many of you have seen a sonogram of an unborn child?

Even if it isn't your own child, watching a sonogram is an absolutely amazing experience. A moving sonogram allows us to glimpse the mystery of creation, the development of new life, inside the womb.

Sometimes we cannot see what God is creating in our lives. Like the young girl in Luke's story, though, God wants us to accept the Divine will as our best future. We just need to accept it and declare, "Let it be."

Storytelling/Scripture Recital

For an optional performance, mute the audio track on the

accompanying storytelling video and accompany the telling with a live instrumental rendition of "What Child Is This," possibly with sonogram special effects played through the sound system.

Prayer

Lord, God of all creation, we give you thanks for the miracle of the conception and birth of your Son. We rejoice at the spirit of Jesus' mother Mary, who willingly accepted your divine future for her life. We open ourselves to receive and give birth to your purpose for our lives. Give us the courage and humility to be like Mary. We surrender all that we have and all that we are to you. Bring to birth what you want in us. Let it be. Amen.

Closing Words/Benediction

May the blessing of God be with you in all the ways Christ is being born in you. Be on the alert for the angel of God speaking to you this week and pay attention to the spirit of God moving within you. And may the peace of God that passes all understanding be with you and abide with you this day and forevermore.

Drama

One possibility is a monologue from Mary's point of view. The setting could be a park, where a young girl slowly swings on a swing, deep in thought. The angel's appearance was earlier in the day. The sketch is the congregation hearing Mary's thoughts as she contemplates what the angel has said, and it ends unresolved. An unresolved ending provides a good segue to a sermon.

Display

A TV monitor with a running sonogram, looping

In Search of ...

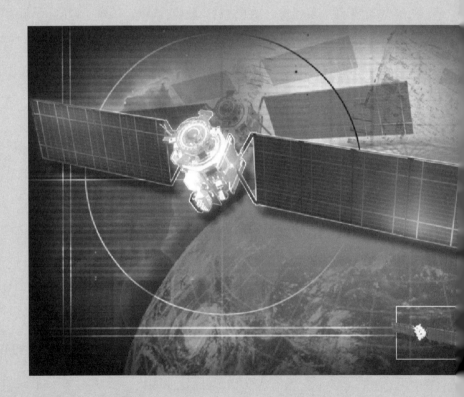

Overview

Discovering that Jesus is the true end of our search for happiness, meaning, and fulfillment

Theme

In Search of…

Metaphor/Image

satellite in deep space

Treatment

Whether they know it or not, people today are searching for God, as they always have. Like satellites that search deep space for answers to the mysteries of the cosmos, the Magi followed the star and found Jesus, the answer to their search for the Messiah.

Human Need

We search for power and peace in the midst of our lives, especially in times of danger and chaos.

Experience

To point people to Jesus as Lord of their world and the answer to their search.

Word

Primary Scripture: Matthew 2:1-12

Lectionary Week

Epiphany, Year A; Isaiah 60:1-6, Psalm 72:1-7, 10-14, Ephesians 3:1-12

Related Scripture

Acts 10:1-33, Mark 5:24-34, 1 Kings 19:11-18, John 1:35-42

Topics

Primary Topics

revelation, Epiphany, mystery, worship, seekers, searching

Related Topics

transformation, light, astrology

Movies

U2: Rattle and Hum (1988)

Plot: A documentary of the 1988 North American tour of the Irish rock band U2.

Clip: Show the clip of a live performance of the song "I Still Haven't Found What I'm Looking For" performed by the rock band U2 with a gospel choir in Harlem.

Time: (VHS) 15:09-19:46, length 4:47

Music

"I Still Haven't Found What I'm Looking For"—U2. '80s hit about searching for answers.

"Drops of Jupiter"—Train. '00s hit. Good for an opener.

"Satellite"—Dave Mathews Band. '90s hit.

"We Three Kings—Christmas hymn.

"Little Drummer Boy"—Christmas song.

Lumiclip Description

The vast, lonely journey of a satellite traveling through space captures the feeling of searching that we feel in our lives. Meditative, cinematic. Running time 1:20

Integration

Sermon Starters

This worship experience focuses on the search of the wise men for the one whose birth had been foretold and heralded by the appearance of a bright star. The magi were probably astrologers. Astrology uses the configurations of the planets, particularly at the time of a person's birth, to make predictions about a person's character and the events that will happen to him or her.

There are several traditions in antiquity of new stars arising in the sky at the time of the birth of great men, such as Alexander the Great and Augustus Caesar (see *The Birth of the Messiah,* by Raymond Brown. Delacorte, 1999, p. 170). The fact that these men come from the East to pay tribute to Jesus confirms his identity as a king. It also represents the fulfillment of God's promise that all nations would recognize the ruler God would send to Israel.

The Greek phrase used to describe the star is ambiguous and can mean either "We have seen his star 'in the east' or 'at its rising.'" In light of the motif of a new star appearing in the sky at the births of great men in antiquity, it is more likely that the meaning is closer to "at its rising."

The elements of the story reflect responses in the ancient world to threats to those in power. Raymond Brown has collected a series of those stories. For example, the Emperor Nero saw a comet for several days and interpret-

ed that as a sign that a contender for the throne was arising. In response, he had several notables executed.
(Brown). Likewise, when the wise men come to Herod to
ask if he knows where to find the child who was born
"King of the Jews," Herod becomes convinced that this
child poses a serious threat to his power and the succession
of his own children to the throne. He consults with the
wise men and with the chief priests and scribes to gather
information, and plots to destroy the child.

However, God intervenes to defeat Herod's plot. Appearing to them a dream, God warns them not to tell Herod
where they have found Jesus. God also appears to Joseph
in a dream warning him to flee with his new family to
Egypt. God is presented in this story as one who is fully
capable of entering into the intrigue of royal politics and
winning.

The interpretive challenge of this story is to communicate
the mystery and wonder of God's actions to save Jesus in
the midst of a climate of political machinations and
intrigue where contenders for the throne are regularly
assassinated. The star, the dreams, and the wise men from
the East all point to Jesus as the Messiah. The story is an
affirmation that Jesus is the King of Israel. At the time
when Matthew was writing his Gospel, around 80 A.D., the
Jewish war of independence had been lost and thousands
of Jews had been killed or taken to Rome as slaves. In part,
the story affirms that Jesus' power does not depend on
what happens politically. It also declares that Jesus is
king—even over the emperors of Rome.

Thus, the story is an answer not only to the people of the
first century but also to people throughout history who
search for a ruler who will bring peace and justice to the

world. The satellite is a contemporary metaphor for the search of the wise men. We send out satellites to search for knowledge and for answers to the mysteries of the stars. The wise men also set out to discover the wondrous event signaled by the appearance of this star. They found the goal of their search in the child Jesus. We can all identify with the quest of the wise men to seek answers to the mysteries of life.

This story connects with the stories of seeking something of supreme value and setting everything else aside in order to pursue that search. It most deeply connects with the stories of those who are searching for God. Whether we are members of a church or "seekers," the story invites us to identify the ways in which we are searching for a deeper knowledge and relationship with God and with Christ.

Call to Worship
Begin with a clip, if appropriate.

In the 1970s, the United States launched the Voyager satellite. Its purpose was to explore deep space in search of answers to the mysteries of the cosmos.

In the first century, the Magi set out in search of the ruler of the cosmos. The star they had seen guided them on their journey.

Our satellites continue to explore the planets and stars of the heavens, but the Magi found what they were looking for in Jesus. If you're searching for God today, you've come to the right place.

Storytelling/Scripture Recital
Tell the story with a sense of adventure and intrigue, remembering that Herod wants to kill the child king.

Using a musical soundtrack for background will enhance the telling of the story of the Magi. You may want to use a portion of a film score from a movie like "Indiana Jones," or a classical piece such as Ravel's "Bolero."

Prayer

Begin the prayer by inviting people to voice some of their fears and concerns about issues around the world as well as at home.

We live in a world torn by political intrigue and terror, around the world and at home. In this climate, we search for peace, for power on which we can depend, and for an authority that we can trust. Lord of heaven and earth, we pray that we might, like the Magi, come to the end of our search and truly see the light of your presence in our lives and in the world. Teach us how to trust you more deeply and to search for you with all that we have and all that we are.

Closing Words/Benediction

May your search lead you to the place of discovery and to the divine presence. May the blessing of the Magi, who searched and found Jesus, be with you this week.

Display

A model satellite, space type items, etc.

Narrow Escape

Overview

Escaping the presence of evil

Theme

Narrow Escape

Metaphor/Image

Shelter from a tornado

Treatment

Terrible things happen in life, and this has been true throughout human history. In this story, we see that Joseph and his family, through God's intervention and guidance, are able to escape Herod's evil intention to destroy Jesus.

Human Need

We need to learn to face our fears. Often people who go through a time of fear come out "on the other side" with a real peace. This rite of passage is a necessary part of dealing with present evil. In times of tragedy, people become more aware of themselves, of life, of what matters. This heightened awareness is a primary function of spirituality. In these moments, we may be able to recognize more clearly what truly matters.

Experience

We are reminded by this story of escape, terror, and return of God's protection and providence in times of fear and danger.

Word

Primary Scripture: Matthew 2:13-23

Lectionary Week

First Sunday after Christmas, Year A; Isaiah 63:7-9, Psalm 148, Hebrews 2:10-18

Related Scripture

Romans 8:28, Genesis 38, Jeremiah 31:15, Hosea 11:1

Topics

Primary Topics

protection, providence, deliverance, evil, fear, murder, death

Related Topics

terror, safety, fatherhood, escape, courage, hardships, loss, pain

Movies

Twister (1996)

Plot: Bill Harding (Bill Paxton) and his wife, Jo (Helen Hunt), are scientists at a university who conduct research on tornados. They begin to have marriage troubles, and Bill decides to leave his marriage and his career. But a series of intense storms draws them back together as they attempt to insert a revolutionary measuring device into a tornado's eye.

Clip: A family runs to their cellar to avoid an oncoming tornado in rural Oklahoma. The clip starts with the changing weather pattern; you will need to dissolve it after they get into the cellar but before the tornado actually strikes.

Time: (VHS) 00:49-3:35, (DVD) Chapter 1 00:49-3:35, length 2:46

Wizard of Oz (1939)

Plot: Dorothy Gale (Judy Garland) decides to run away from her rural Kansas home after a nasty neighbor threatens to have her dog put to sleep. But she finds herself caught in a terrible storm and is swept away by a tornado to the magical land of Oz. She sets out to see the Wizard, who is the one who can help her find her way back home.

Clip: The ranch hands scramble around as the twister can be seen coming on the horizon. End is optional.

Time: (VHS) 15:01-17:04, length 2:03

Life is Beautiful (*La Vita è Bella*) (1997)

Plot: Jewish waiter Guido Orefice (Roberto Benigni) falls in love with a beautiful woman, Dora, whom he finally wins over with his charm and humor. Five years later when the Germans occupy Italy, Guido and his family are imprisoned in a Nazi death camp. Guido does everything in his power to protect his young son from the truth about their dire situation by convincing him that they are involved in an elaborate game, and that the winner gets a tank.

NOTE: If using the DVD version of this film, you may choose the English-language-dubbed version for easier understandability in worship.

Clip: Orefice hides his son in a metal crate on the last night at a Nazi concentration camp. Best used in conjunction with second clip.

Time: (VHS) 1:39:38-1:41:05, (DVD) Ch. 26, 1:07-2:34, length 1:27

Clip: The next morning, the boy comes out of the crate to an empty, liberated camp. The unseen aspect of the clip is that the boy's father gave his life for him. End with the boy walking about the courtyard by himself.

Time: (VHS) 1:47:04-1:49:35, (DVD) Ch. 26, 8:03-10:34, length 2:31

The Patriot (2000)

Plot: Benjamin Martin (Mel Gibson), an officer who fought bravely in the French and Indian War, vows to remain home with his children after his wife's death rather than join the fight against the British. Against his will, he finds himself drawn into the conflict after a brutal British commander kills his son. He vows to avenge the death of his son and protect the life of his oldest son who has also joined the fight.

Clip: When the British army comes to sack the Martin plantation home, the family hides in the basement kitchen. One boy doesn't make it downstairs in time, and must elude a soldier searching the dining room. Begin with the troops approaching the house and end with the boy behind the table.

Time: (VHS) 1:38:59-1:41:24, (DVD) Chapter 20, 1:10-3:35, length 2:25

The Sound of Music (1965)

Plot: Maria (Julie Andrews), a young nun, is sent from her convent to be a governess for the children of a widowed Naval officer (Christopher Plummer). The Mother Superior arranges this opportunity so that Maria can experience the real world before she takes her vows.

Clip: The von Trapp family hides in a convent to avoid detection by the Nazis.

Time: (VHS) 2:44:47-2:48:29, (DVD) Chapter 57, 0:00-
3:42, length 3:42

Music

"The Impression That I Get"—Mighty Mighty Bosstones.
This '90s hit makes a good opener.

"Shelter from the Storm"—Bob Dylan. Perfect for a feature. Your relationship with Christ can sustain you
through times of spiritual change and conflict.

"I Will Call Upon the Lord"—Contemporary praise.

"Trading My Sorrows"—Contemporary praise.

"You Are My Hiding Place"—Praise song.

"He Leadeth Me"—hymn.

"Stand By Me"—hymn.

Integration

Sermon Starters

This story of Jesus' escape from Herod's slaughter of the
male infants of Bethlehem is frequently ignored in the celebration of Christmas because it seems so contradictory to
the spirit of the season. No one wants to hear about exe-
cutions of babies at the time when we are enjoying the
warm fuzzies of Christmas. But, for Matthew's listeners in
the first century, and potentially for us, this story places the
birth of the Messiah in the context of the realities of life
and gives spiritual credibility and depth to the story.

By contrast, the primary meaning of Christmas has
become the buying and giving of presents. The story of the
narrow escape of Joseph and his family from Herod's jeal-
ous slaughter of Bethlehem's children sets Christmas in the

context of political conflict, hatred, violence, jealousy, and the deaths of innocent children.

Matthew makes several connections between Jesus' childhood experience and Israel's experiences of narrow escape. The patriarch Joseph, Israel's son, was sold into slavery in Egypt, but through God's interventions, became the means by which the tribe of Israelites escaped famine in the land of Caanan. The baby Moses narrowly escaped being killed when Pharaoh commanded the Israelite midwives to kill any boy baby they delivered (Ex. 1:15ff.). In the exodus of the Israelites from Egypt, God delivered the people from slavery and death and brought them back to the Promised Land in Caanan. Jesus' early life was, therefore, a recapitulation of the experience of Israel. Matthew presents these stories as the fulfillment of Scripture and as a sign that Jesus is Israel's long-awaited Messiah.

It may be helpful to clarify the chronology of Jesus' life in Matthew's story, since we often see Christmas pageants where the wise men present their gifts to the infant Jesus at the same time as the announcement to the shepherds. In Matthew, Jesus was most likely between one and two years old when the magi arrive from the East. Although this is not explicitly stated in the text, this is implied by the fact that Herod takes great interest in finding out from the wise men exactly when the star appeared and ordered the killing of the boys two years of age and under. Herod dies only a couple of years after Joseph and his family narrowly escaped to Egypt. This would mean that Jesus is between three and five years old when the family finally settles in Nazareth.

The slaughter of the boys of Bethlehem is a poignant story of innocent children and their families caught in the crossfire of political conflict. It is particularly painful because these little boys die as a result of the political conflict generated by Jesus' birth while Jesus escapes. It is a classic instance of innocent suffering that accompanies the accomplishment of God's purposes. They are appropriately celebrated as martyrs in the Church's traditional observance of this day.

Jesus, like the other Bethlehem boys of his generation, also dies—but only after he has accomplished the mission of bringing salvation to the nation of Israel and to the world. This story, like the death of John the Baptist, foreshadows Jesus' suffering and death in a later crossfire of political and religious conflict.

At this time, however, Jesus' two fathers, God and Joseph, work together to protect this little boy. God protects and delivers God's son. Joseph listens to God and acts decisively to save his son's life in the midst of the political developments of his time. He is a model for all fathers of spiritual sensitivity and wise action.

Furthermore, the story honors the grief of the mothers of Bethlehem by setting their grief in the context of God's providence. These deaths are not meaningless. They become part of the larger action of God's salvation. This provides a context for the grieving of all parents who lose their babies. Furthermore, the deaths of innocent children, which happen with such painful regularity—even in Jesus' hometown of Bethlehem—are caught up in the reality of God's ongoing providence and love. This story proclaims that God will use these deaths as a means of carrying out God's purpose of salvation for all.

In different ways, each of the movies listed in the film clips, with the exception of *The Wizard of Oz*, also tells a story of a narrow escape in the midst of the deaths of innocent persons. Both the escapes and the deaths become part of a larger story of deliverance from the powers of sin and death.

Call to Worship

Begin with a clip if one is available.

When a tornado is coming, people flee to the safety of a storm shelter. When the wrath of Herod threatened, the angel told Joseph to take his family to the safety of Egypt.

Where do you feel safe when you are afraid? What are the tornados, the terrors, of your life? Where would you go if they were to come? Today, let's spend some time in Joseph's shoes and consider what he must have been thinking and feeling. God helped Joseph to protect the infant Jesus, just as Jesus now protects us. Let's worship the God of narrow escapes together.

Prayer

In an atmosphere of safety, invite people to name their fears—their worst nightmares, their personal experiences of terror. Then lead them through a guided meditation where they can visualize being protected by a guardian angel as Joseph was. Allow them the freedom to hear comfort and safety from God through their angel.

Closing Words/Benediction

May God protect you and help you escape the terrors of life. And May the peace of God that passes all understanding be with you and abide with you, this day and forevermore. Amen.

Other

Invite someone in the congregation to give a personal testimony about going through a time of terror, but feeling protected and sustained by God's presence.

Can I play a DVD on My Computer, Projector, or TV?

For the computer, in addition to a DVD-ROM drive you must have **either** a) extra hardware to decode MPEG-2 video and Dolby Digital or MPEG-2 audio, **or** b) your computer must be fast enough to handle software decoding. Good quality software-only playback requires a 350-MHz Pentium II or a Mac G4. Less than ten percent of new computers with DVD-ROM drives include decoder hardware, since software decoding is now possible on even the cheapest new models. Hardware upgrade kits can be purchased for existing older computers (usually with a minimum 133 MHz Pentium or G3), starting at $150. See <u>http://www.dvddemystified.com/dvdfaq></u> for an exhaustive list of commonly asked questions and answers about DVD.

Three graphics files for each worship experience can also be found in a separate folder on the DVD-ROM disk. These files are, of course, only accessible from a computer and not from a stand-alone DVD player.

In our test environment we determined that the DVD plays well from a set-top DVD player that is connected to a TV or video projector. Instead of using a computer mouse, you will use the DVD player's remote control to select the on-screen buttons that play and navigate through the DVD. When using one of the video clips, you will most likely cue it prior to worship and press play at the appropriate moment. The video clips are not available separately in a graphics folder.

Abingdon Press technical support is available to assist you by answering questions that pertain directly to the interface for this product. We are not equipped, however, to provide technical support for your DVD player, audio or video software codecs, or for your computer operating system. If operating in Microsoft Windows, outdated drivers are the biggest cause of problems. You are encouraged to go to <u>http://windowsupdate.microsoft.com/></u> to make sure that you have the latest audio, graphics, and video drivers for your system. If you suspect systems or hardware issues, or have experienced issues with other disks, please go to <u>http://www.dvddemystified.com/dvdfaq></u>, especially paragraph 4.6, for further help.

Abingdon technical support can be reached at (615) 749-6777, Monday through Friday, 8 AM to 5 PM, Central Standard Time.

Help Screen for DVD

BACK

To view the image as a full screen, select the image icon by using the arrow keys on the remote control. Then click "OK" on the remote control.

To play video clip, select video clip icon using the arrow keys on the remote control, and then click "OK" on the remote control.

To move to the next experience select the "NEXT MENU" button on screen and click "OK" on the remote control.

To return to the menu from the full screen image or the video clip, click "MENU" on the remote control.

To return to the main menu, click the "DISK" button on the remote control, or select the "MAIN MENU" button on screen by using arrow keys on the remote control, and then click "OK" on the remote control.